# The

Our Father which art in heaven,
Hallowed be thy Name.
Thy kingdom come.
Thy will be done in earth,
as it is in heaven.
Give us this day our daily bread.
And forgive us our debts, as we
forgive our debtors.  And lead
us not into temptation,
but deliver us from evil: For
thine is the kingdom,
and the power, and the
glory, for ever.
Amen.
Matthew 6:9-13 KJV

# Jesus

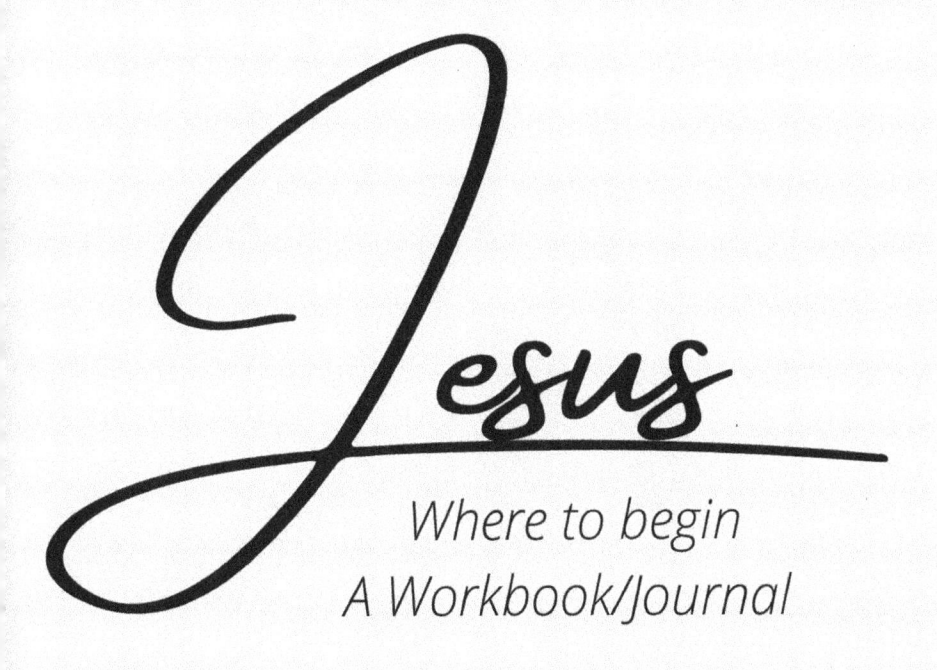

*Where to begin*
*A Workbook/Journal*

◆ FriesenPress

One Printers Way
Altona, MB R0G 0B0
Canada

www.friesenpress.com

Copyright © 2024 by Terri Lynn Godwin
First Edition — 2024

All rights reserved.

All scriptures have been taken from The Authorized King James Version, World Bible Publishers.

No part of this publication may be reproduced in any form, or by any means, electronic or mechanical, including photocopying, recording, or any information browsing, storage, or retrieval system, without permission in writing from FriesenPress.

ISBN
978-1-03-918021-5 (Hardcover)
978-1-03-918020-8 (Paperback)
978-1-03-918022-2 (eBook)

1. Religion, Christian Living, Devotional Journal

Distributed to the trade by The Ingram Book Company

*This book belongs to*

_____

*Date*

_____

# Who Is Jesus?

Jesus saith unto him,
I am the WAY, the TRUTH, and the LIFE: No man cometh unto the Father, but by me.  John 14:6

## THE WAY

As for God, His way is perfect; the Word of the Lord is tried: He is a buckler to all them that trust in Him.
2 Samuel 22:31
In the way of righteousness is life; and in the pathway thereof there is no death.
Proverbs 12:28

## THE TRUTH

For the Word of the Lord is right; and all His works are done in truth.
Psalm 33:4
And the Word was made flesh, and dwelt among us, (and we beheld His glory, the glory as of the only begotten of the Father,) full of grace and truth.
John 1:14

## THE LIFE

I am come that they might have life, and that they might have it more abundantly.
John 10:10
Thou wilt shew me the path of life: in thy presence is fulness of joy; at thy right hand there are pleasures for evermore.
Psalm 16:11

---

Thou art my hiding place and my shield: I hope in thy Word.  Psalm 119:114

# Are You Saved?

*Jesus answered and said unto him, Verily, verily I say unto thee, Except a man be born again, he cannot see the kingdom of God.*
John 3:3

Are you born again? This is your first step. If you do not have a church and desire to change your life and give your heart to Jesus, you can search for Pentecostal or non-denominational churches in your area and see how you feel about their mission statement. Does it speak to your heart?

Becoming a child of God. This is life-changing. Forever. For all of eternity. We are immortal beings, and where we spend eternity is up to us. Salvation, however, can only happen through faith.

We must believe that He is. That He exists.

Making our confession before the God of the whole universe, the creator of everything good, including you, is the most POWERFUL thing that you will do in your entire life. How could our glorious God, your creator, not love you? He is the one who made you, you. And He is waiting for you to come home. Building your faith is an everyday event. Worship, prayer, and reading His Word along with attending church will teach you the truth about who He is and what He can do in your life.

*Who hath saved us, and called us with an holy calling, not according to our works, but according to His own purpose and grace, which was given us in Christ Jesus before the world began, But is now made manifest by the appearing of our Saviour Jesus Christ, who hath abolished death, and hath brought life and immortality to light through the gospel:*
2 Timothy 1:9-10

---

For God so loved the world, that He gave His only begotten Son, that whosoever believeth in Him should not perish, but have everlasting life. John 3:16

Be strong and of good courage;
be not afraid,
neither be thou dismayed:
for the Lord thy God is with thee
whithersoever thou goest.
Joshua 1:9

# Welcome

## YOU ARE LOVED
## AND YOU
## HAVE A PURPOSE

and you were created by God for a very good reason. You are the only one who can do the things God has designed for you. Your friendship and your talent are what He is waiting for. He has plans for you, and He wants you to know that there is goodness in your life and all around you. His perfect goodness. He wants you to find this goodness. His desire is for you to live in His joy and peace every day: the good days, the bad days, and all the days in between. Let's start looking for the good and appreciating His love for us. All you need is the Holy Bible (I recommend the King James Bible), your time, and the twelve pages per month, which are designed for journalling and for keeping track of the good things that are happening all around you, as your faith grows daily.

Finding your church family (if you haven't yet), is very important. This is the place where you'll find and practice love and support. Get to know your brothers and sisters in Christ. Practicing patience and loving-kindness, as well as receiving them, is beautiful.

Now, through reading the Word, prayer, and worship you will find new meaning in your life, all while learning to walk in faith with Jesus Christ, your beautiful Saviour.

> I will praise thee; for I am fearfully and
> wonderfully made: Psalm 139:14

# TABLE OF CONTENTS

## WELCOME — 1

## BE TEACHABLE — 4
Til I come, give attendance to reading, to exhortation, to doctrine.  1 Timothy 4:13

## OH GLORIOUS DAY — 6
I will never leave thee, nor forsake thee. Hebrews 13:5

## PRAYER — 7
Praying always with all prayer and supplication in the Spirit, and watching thereunto with all perseverance and supplication for all saints;  Ephesians 6:18

## MY TIME — 8
Study to shew thyself approved unto God, a workman that needeth not to be ashamed, rightly dividing the Word of truth.  2 Timothy 2:15

## WORDS ARE POWERFUL — 9
Let thine heart retain my words: keep my commandments, and live.  Proverbs 4:4

## WISDOM — 10
In whom are hid all the treasures of wisdom and knowledge. Colossians 2:3

## THE HOLY WORD OF GOD — 11
but my heart standeth in awe of thy Word. Psalm 119:161

# TABLE OF CONTENTS

## FAVOURITE SCRIPTURES   14

Thy Word is a lamp unto my feet, and a light unto my path.  Psalm 119:105

## WORSHIP MUSIC   15

O come, let us sing unto the Lord: let us make a joyful noise to the rock of our salvation.  Psalm 95:1

## QUESTIONS   18

And whatsoever we ask, we receive of Him, because we keep His commandments, and do those things that are pleasing in His sight.  1 John 3:22

## FORGIVE.   22

In whom we have redemption through His blood, the forgiveness of sins, according to the riches of His grace;  Ephesians 1:7

## LETTING GO   24

Stand fast therefore in the liberty wherewith Christ hath made us free, and be not entangled again with the yoke of bondage.  Galatians 5:1

## PUTTING THOUGHT INTO MY THOUGHTS   26

Thou wilt keep him in perfect peace, whose mind is stayed on thee: because he trusteth in thee.  Isaiah 26:3

## KEEPING ON TRACK JOURNALLING PAGES   30

# Be teachable

> But the anointing which ye have received of Him abideth in you, and ye need not that any man teach you: but as the same anointing teacheth you of all things, and is truth and is no lie, and even as it hath taught you, ye shall abide in Him.
> 1 John 2:27

Through His Word we get to know Him and His perfect, selfless love. And again, through His love, we discover who we are, and who He created us to be. The perfect version of ourselves.

> But let patience have her perfect work, that ye may be perfect and entire, wanting nothing.
> James 1:4

Digging deep into His Word is like digging deep into His love for us. We see His perfect grace and mercy in our lives and His patience and longsuffering toward us all as we explore and learn who we are in Him.

This takes time, precious time. The time you spend with Him becomes something you run to. You can't wait to feel His love as you let everything go, leaving all of the stress and worry of the day at His feet in prayer, for the sole purpose of basking in the glow of His love. Desire His love deep in your soul. It changes us and fills us with His perfect peace and contentment. Trust His Word, expect the unexpected in every area of your life, put your faith in Him in everything, and watch it grow. Let's get to know Him a little better today.

Praise God and give Him all the glory!

> But thou, o Lord, art a God full of compassion, and gracious, longsuffering, and plenteous in mercy and truth.   Psalm 86:15

for the joy of the Lord is your strength.
Nehemiah 8:10

## I belong.
## My life is hidden with Christ in God.

## How do you get to know Jesus?

Well, first you take a deep breath, let it go, relax,. . . .and then you open your heart and invite Him in. The key is to open your whole heart, *yes*, even the parts *you* don't want to see. Jesus is your friend.

*but I have called you friends;*
*John 15:15*

He is waiting to shine the light of His love into the deepest, darkest parts of your heart. Let Him in and let it all go.

Find freedom.

Find joy and peace.

Find the love your heart and soul have been searching for your whole life.

Now the God of hope fill you with all joy and peace in believing, that ye may abound in hope, through the power of the Holy Ghost.  Romans 15:13

# O Glorious Day

Waking up with joy in my heart. Is this possible for me? I'm taking a deep breath, and as I exhale slowly I feel all of my muscles relax.

Let everything go.

Where to?

To the feet of my Saviour.

PRAY

He takes my burdens from me and He replaces them with joy and peace. This day I will walk with my Saviour and remember:

I am a child of God
I do not walk in fear
I walk in faith.

---

*Rejoice ye in that day, and leap for joy: for, behold, your reward is great in heaven: Luke 6:23*

# Prayer

All that You are is so overwhelming. Your love, grace, and mercy in my life, is my comfort; it is my joy and peace. I will lay everything at Your feet in faith as I praise Your holy name and give all the glory to You, my King and my Saviour. I ask forgiveness for my sins, and I ask for Your help in having a good and loving attitude so that my life will be filled with Your beautiful Holy Spirit, remembering always, wherever I am, that I am never alone. You are walking with me. Thank you.
In Jesus' name, Amen.

Be careful for nothing; but in every thing by prayer and supplication with thanksgiving let your requests be made known unto God.   Philippians 4:6

# My Time

The simple truth is, the more time you spend on something, the more you go through, the more effort you put in to it, the more it's going to mean to you. And truly, the only way to get to know someone or something is by offering your time.

Your time is of the utmost importance, particularly when it comes to getting to know Him; Jesus, your loving and faithful Saviour. These precious moments that you are going to spend alone with Him will help you to build a relationship that forms a firm, lasting foundation that you can forever stand on, depend on, and trust. Your faith will grow stronger and stronger as you see Him moving in your life.

Even if all you have to spare is ten minutes in prayer and ten minutes in the Word before your day starts, that's okay. Creating daily time with Jesus helps us to grow and stay strong in our walk of faith.

---

Take my yoke upon you, and learn of me; for I am meek and lowly in heart: and ye shall find rest unto your souls.  Matthew 11:29

# Words Are Powerful

God spoke the earth into existence, as well as every living thing on the planet. Words Are Powerful. Once spoken, there is no turning back. Filling your life with positive influences will go a long way to holding on to a positive attitude. Speak goodness and love into your life. Read the Word out loud. Fill the air with worship music, and try as much as possible to stay away from negative influences.

Just a reminder

As your faith grows, the peace in your life will begin to replace the fear of the unknown. Why?

Because God knows.

---

Whoso keepeth his mouth and his tongue keepeth his soul from troubles. Proverbs 21:23

# Wisdom

So that thou incline thine ear unto wisdom, and apply thine heart to understanding; Yea, if thou criest after knowledge, and liftest up thy voice for understanding; If thou seekest her as silver, and searchest for her as for hid treasures; then shalt thou understand the fear of the Lord, and find the knowledge of God. For the Lord giveth wisdom: out of His mouth cometh knowledge and understanding. He layeth up sound wisdom for the righteous: He is a buckler to them that walk uprightly. He keepeth the paths of judgement, and preserveth the way of His saints. Then shalt thou understand righteousness, judgment, and equity; yea, every good path. When wisdom entereth into thine heart, and knowledge is pleasant unto thy soul; discretion shall preserve thee, understanding shall keep thee:
Proverbs 2:2-11

Consider what I say; and the Lord give thee understanding in all things.  2 Timothy 2:7

# The Holy Word of God

# Walking in the Truth

Read the Word of God. Because when you have the truth in your heart, you know it.

**PARDES**

This is the Hebrew word for Bible; it means garden or paradise.

PARDES is an acronym describing the four levels of understanding in the Word of God,

P'Shat - Simple
Remez - Implied
Drash - Deeper
Sod - Hidden

The Word of God is deep. When changed, the depth of the scriptures can be lost.

In the beginning was the Word, and the Word was with God, and the Word was God. The same was in the beginning with God. All things were made by Him; and without Him was not anything made that was made. In Him was life; and the life was the light of men.
John 1:1-4 KJV

Sanctify them through thy truth: thy Word is truth. John 17:17

> For the Word of God is quick, and powerful, and sharper than any two-edged sword, piercing even to the dividing asunder of soul and spirit, and of the joints and marrow, and is a discerner of the thoughts and intents of the heart.
> Hebrews 4:12

What happens when you open up the holy Word of God? You find life, you find love, and you come home to the place your soul has been waiting for, for a long time.

Learning about Jesus is learning about love. It's rich and filled with everything we need to navigate our way through life (not an easy task at any age). We have to fight to find our way through a world where the truth is relative to opinion and sin is celebrated. Read the Bible, knowing in the depths of your soul that you are reading the truth, and our God is goodness, light, and love.

the goodness of God endureth continually.
Psalms 52:1

That your faith should not stand in the wisdom of men, but in the power of God. 1 Corinthians 2:5

# Favourite Scriptures

As for God, His way is perfect: the Word of the Lord is tried: He is a buckler to all those that trust in Him.   Psalm 18:30

# Worship Music

Praise ye the Lord. Praise God in His sancuary: praise Him in the firmament of His power.
Psalm 150:1

# Praise Music Changes the Day

It is a good thing to give thanks unto the Lord, and to sing praises unto thy name, O most high: To shew forth thy lovingkindness in the morning, and thy faithfulness every night, Psalm 92:1-2

Make a joyful noise unto the Lord, all the earth: make a loud noise, and rejoice, and sing praise.
Psalm 98:4

# Praise and Worship

When you begin to praise the Lord, something happens, something changes. Our hearts become softer and the love of God fills us with joy and the most beautiful peace. Sometimes, praise and worship can seem difficult for, well, many reasons (we all have hard times), when He seems too far away, or maybe something we have done is playing with our minds and creating havoc, causing us to feel unworthy of even being able to praise Him, do it anyway.

Turn on the radio. Find a Christian station, or use an app and create different types of playlists. You can start with a list for daytime, with joyful, happy Christian songs playing in the background. You can have another list of favourite worship songs to play in the morning before prayer, to help you feel closer to His beautiful, glorious Spirit even before you get on your knees.

*From the rising of the sun unto the going down of the same the Lord's name is to be praised.*
Psalm 113:3

# Questions?

How many life questions do you have?

Let's go on a quest for some truth-telling, life-changing answers.

What's it all about?

Who am I?

Who is God  and  Who is He to me?

How can I have a relationship with Jesus?

How will this relationship change my life?

Some of these you will only be able to answer once you have spent some time with Him.

---

And ye shall seek me, and find me, when ye shall search for me with all your heart.   Jeremiah 29:13

*For the Lord is good; His mercy is everlasting; and His truth endureth to all generations.   Psalm 100:5*

# Some Truths

Start with some truths about how you feel.

Why am I here?   What is my life purpose?

Do I have faith to trust in His Word?

What does the Lord God Almighty require of me?

    And he answering said,

Thou shalt love the Lord thy God with all thy heart, and with all thy soul, and with all thy strength, and with all thy mind; and thy neighbor as thyself.   Luke 10:27

You see, all He requires is love.

What are some of your own life questions?

*Ye shall know the truth, and the truth shall make you free.   John 8:32*

# QUESTIONS

# THOUGHTS

# FORGIVE.

Forgiveness is life-changing. Learning to let go of hurt and anger is only challenging if you are trying to do it on your own. We have freedom in Christ. Give the feelings you think you have no control over to Him in prayer, and have faith. Don't forget to add yourself to this list; we must forgive ourselves as well. We all make mistakes. His love conquers all.

Forbearing one another, and forgiving one another, if any man have a quarrel against any: even as Christ forgave you, so also do ye.
Colossians 3:13

And be ye kind one to another, tenderhearted, forgiving one another, even as God for Christ's sake hath forgiven you.
Ephesians 4:32

## Remember

I can do all things

through Christ which

strengtheneth me.

Philippians 4:13

---

As far as the east is from the west, so far hath he removed our transgressions from us.  Psalm 103:12

# How do I feel about forgiving others and myself?

Remember you are already forgiven by your Saviour.

Write about forgiveness whenever you feel like you need to let something go. Sometimes, just writing it down and giving it to Jesus helps. You can also write it on a separate piece of paper and throw it away to help with closure.

_____

_____

_____

_____

_____

_____

_____

_____

_____

_____

_____

_____

_____

*and the prayer of faith shall save the sick, and the Lord shall raise him up; and if he have committed sins, they shall be forgiven him.* James 5:15

# Letting Go

When we carry the difficult things of this life, all the stress, and worry, all the heartache, and unforgiveness, we tend to be tense most of the time. Holding on to all the troubles and cares of this life is killing us, or at the very least robbing us of the joy that is truly within reach. It's weighing us down to the point of exhaustion. This is why we begin with breathing. We can't let anything go if we are living in tension and worry.

So
breathe
in
slowly
breathe
out
slowly.
Again
and
again.

Feel yourself relax. If you need to, think about each of your muscle groups and consciously feel them letting go of any tension.

Let it all go.

---

For His merciful kindness is great toward us: and the truth of the Lord endureth for ever. Praise ye the Lord.
Psalm 117:2

Thus saith the Lord, thy redeemer, and He that formed thee from the womb, I am the Lord that maketh all things; that stretcheth forth the heavens alone; that spreadeth abroad the earth by myself; Isaiah 44:24

---

When you begin to feel your muscles relax, try to do the same with your worries. God is the creator of this world. He spoke the earth into existence.

## God is in control.

Let everything go, even if there is no solution in sight. Give your cares to Him. He will take them from you.

# PRAY

Leave everything at His feet. Be open with Him, talk to Him about the problems you are facing, and simply ask for His help.

> Let us therefore come BOLDLY
> unto the throne of grace, that we
> may obtain mercy, and find grace
> to help in time of need.
> Hebrews 4:16

---

And God said, Let there be light: and there was light.   Genesis 1:3

# Putting Thought into My Thoughts

What we spend our thought time on is often what determines our mood.  When you are at rest or just drifting off, where do your thoughts go?  How blessed your life is, or does worry saturate your thinking?  Do you feel that life is a blessing and should be celebrated, or worry that you're never going to be good enough or will never measure up to the expectations of others?  Maybe you're striving to be better than a co-worker or a sibling, or you're envious of another's blessings.  Strife and envy are not of God.  They are the enemy trying to keep you down.

> For where envying and strife is, there is confusion and every evil work.  James 3:16

Worrying over everything is unbearable.  Striving to be better than others will rob us of the joy that our glorious God has for us right now.

## Let It Go

---

For He satisfieth the longing soul, and filleth the hungry soul with goodness.  Psalm 107:9

Explore every thought as it comes, investigate it when you have time, and talk to Jesus, asking for His help to overcome.

### He will help you.

Ask yourself: "Why am I putting so much pressure on myself? Is it for me, or is it for someone else?"

What about the pressures of the society we live in? Do you feel like you need to be perfect?

### Give all of this to Jesus.

Replace any negative thought that comes with your favourite scripture, or just start praising the Lord. Generally speaking, I say the name of Jesus and cut negative thoughts off completely. Be patient with yourself; nothing happens overnight. It will take time to recognize that those thoughts are taking over. One day, you will notice that instead of fighting off negative thoughts, you just simply start praising the Lord. You might even notice an involuntary smile, realizing that faith came in before fear.

# Hallelujah!

---

Commit thy works unto the Lord, and thy thoughts shall be established. Proverbs 16:3

# THOUGHTS

# THOUGHTS

to give unto them beauty for ashes, the oil of joy for mourning, the garment of praise for the spirit of heaviness;   Isaiah 61:3

## Finding Peace

When I feel overrun and worry is taking over my thoughts, I need to
## fix my eyes on Jesus.

| | | |
|---|---|---|
| Go for a walk | Meditate on my favorite scripture | Listen to praise music AND SING |
| Pick a bouquet of wild flowers | PRAY | Mail a note card to someone just to say hi. |
| Worship the Lord God Almighty | Create a scripture picture. Hang it up. | Journal the Word |

MONTH

Peace I leave with you, my peace I give unto you: not as the world giveth, give I unto you.  Let not your heart be troubled, neither let it be afraid.   John 14:27

Therefore my heart is glad, and my glory rejoiceth: my flesh also shall rest in hope.   Psalm 16:9

# TEA TIME

Take time to rest in His gentle loving-kindness. Slowly take a deep breath.  As you exhale allow your muscles to relax and let go.  Praise God. Thank you, my Lord, that I can leave all of my burdens and cares at Your feet.  You are forever faithful. Please help me keep You close to my heart and always remember that I am a child of God and I walk in faith, not fear.

Now, have your favourite beverage, and enjoy the Word of God, slowly, carefully, and thoughtfully.

If you are unsure where to begin, you can start in the Gospels, the first four books in the New Testament, or choose a scripture from one of these pages, digging deeper, and exploring the surrounding scriptures.

### Notes

_____
_____
_____
_____
_____
_____

Return unto thy rest, O my soul; for the Lord hath dealt bountifully with thee.   Psalm 116:7

# The Goodness of God

## Noticing Goodness Every Day

Monday
------------------------------
------------------------------
------------------------------
------------------------------

Tuesday
------------------------------
------------------------------
------------------------------
------------------------------

Wednesday
------------------------------
------------------------------
------------------------------
------------------------------

Thursday
------------------------------
------------------------------
------------------------------
------------------------------

Friday
------------------------------
------------------------------
------------------------------
------------------------------

Saturday
------------------------------
------------------------------
------------------------------
------------------------------

Sunday
------------------------------
------------------------------
------------------------------
------------------------------

the earth is full of the goodness of the Lord. Psalm 33:5

# With a Grateful Heart

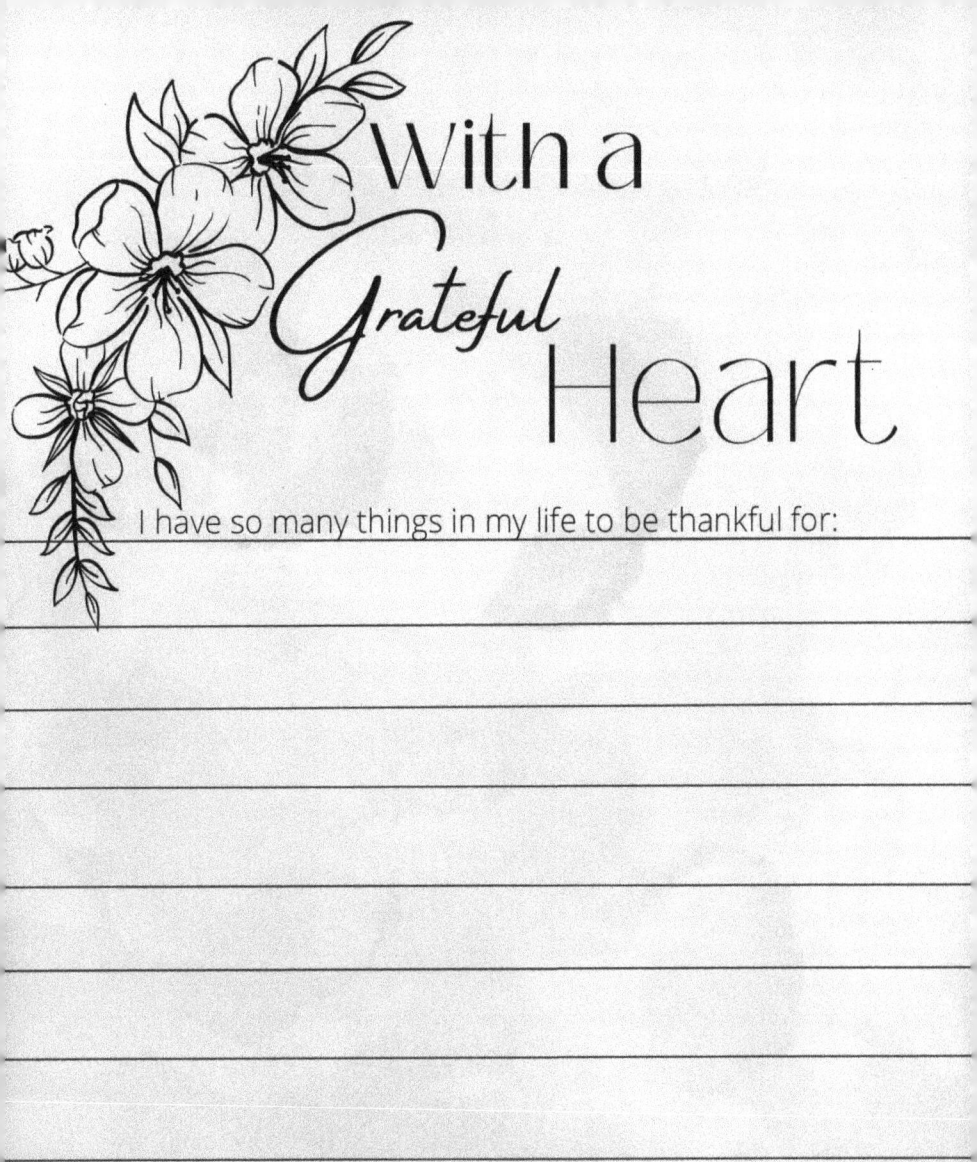

I have so many things in my life to be thankful for:

---

Rooted and built up in Him, and stablished in the faith, as ye have been taught, abounding therein with thanksgiving.
Colossians 2:7

# It's time to pray

## New Prayer Requests

## Answered Prayers

## My Daily Prayers

For the eyes of the Lord are over the righteous, and His ears are open unto their prayers:  1 Peter 3:12

I rejoice at thy Word as one that findeth great spoil.
Psalm 119:162

# FIVE-MINUTE THOUGHTS
## ABOUT MY WALK

FAVOURITE SCRIPTURES

- 
- 
- 
- 

GREAT WORSHIP SONGS

- 
- 
- 
- 

Whether therefore ye eat, or drink, or
whatsoever ye do, do all to the glory of God.
1 Corinthians 10:31

For by grace are ye saved through faith; and that not of yourselves: it is the gift of God:
Ephesians 2:8

# FAITH
# *Builders*

I see the Lord moving in my life:

_____

_____

_____

_____

_____

_____

_____

_____

_____

_____

_____

(For we walk by faith, not by sight:)
2 Corinthians 5:7

# Create

Create in me a clean heart, O God; and renew a right spirit within me.   Psalm 51:10

And we know that all things work together for good to them that love God, to them who are the called according to His purpose.
Romans 8:28

Consider: All things work together for good.

# THOUGHTS

# THOUGHTS

# THOUGHTS

But the fruit of the Spirit is love, joy, peace, longsuffering, gentleness, goodness, faith, meekness, temperance: against such there is no law.
Galatians 5:22-23

# The Fruit of the Spirit

## GOD IS LOVE
1 John 4:16

| LOVE | JOY | PEACE |
|---|---|---|
| LONG-SUFFERING | GENTLENESS | GOODNESS |
| FAITH | MEEKNESS | TEMPERANCE |

MONTH

(For the fruit of the spirit is in all goodness and rightousness and truth;)  Ephesians 5:9

Who comforteth us in all our tribulation, that we may be able to comfort them which are in any trouble, by the comfort wherewith we ourselves are comforted of God.   2 Corinthians 1:4

# TEA TIME

Take time to rest in His gentle loving-kindness. Slowly take a deep breath. As you exhale allow your muscles to relax and let go. Praise God. Thank you, my Lord, that I can leave all of my burdens and cares at Your feet. You are forever faithful. Please help me to keep You close to my heart and always remember that I am a child of God and I walk in faith, not fear.

Now, have your favourite beverage, and enjoy the Word of God, slowly, carefully, and thoughtfully.

Continue in the New Testament, reading John 1, 2, and 3, and Thessalonians 1 and 2 or choose a scripture from one of these pages, digging deeper, and exploring the surrounding scriptures.

NOTES

_____
_____
_____
_____
_____
_____

Ask, and it shall be given you; seek, and ye shall find; knock, and it shall be opened unto you:
Matthew 7:7

# The Goodness of God

## Noticing Goodness Every Day

Monday

Tuesday

Wednesday

Thursday

Friday

Saturday

Sunday

*the goodness of God endureth continually.*
Psalm 52:1

# With a *Grateful* Heart

I have so many things in my life to be thankful for:

> Enter into His gates with thanksgiving, and into His courts with praise: be thankful unto Him, and bless His name.  Psalm 100:4

# It's time to pray

## New Prayer Requests

## Answered Prayers

## My Daily Prayers

Hear my prayer, O Lord, give ear to my supplications: in thy faithfulness answer me, and in thy righteousness. Psalm 143:1

A merry heart doeth good like medicine: but a broken spirit drieth the bones.   Proverbs 17:22

# FIVE-MINUTE THOUGHTS

## ABOUT MY WALK

| FAVOURITE SCRIPTURES | GREAT WORSHIP SONGS |
|---|---|
| . | . |
| . | . |
| . | . |
| . | . |

Thou hast turned for me my mourning into dancing: thou hast put off my sackcloth, and girded me with gladness; To the end that my glory may sing praise to thee, and not be silent.  O Lord my God, I will give thanks unto thee for ever.  Psalm 30:11-12

If ye have faith as a grain of mustard seed, ye shall say unto this mountain, Remove hence to yonder place; and it shall remove; and nothing shall be impossible unto you.
Matthew 17:20

# FAITH
*Builders*

I see the Lord moving in my life:

_____
_____
_____
_____
_____
_____
_____
_____
_____
_____
_____
_____

Daughter, be of good comfort; thy faith has made thee whole. And the woman was made whole from that hour. Matthew 9:22

# Express yourself

Who being the brightness of His glory, and the express image of His person, and upholding all things by the word of His power, when He had by Himself purged our sins, sat down on the right hand of the Majesty on high;   Hebrews 1:3

Therefore if any man be in Christ, he is a new creature: old things are passed away; behold, all things are become new.
2 Corinthians 5:17

Consider: Old things are passed away; all things become new.

# THOUGHTS

# THOUGHTS

# THOUGHTS

For therein is the righteousness of God revealed from faith to faith: as it is written, The just shall live by faith.   Romans 1:17

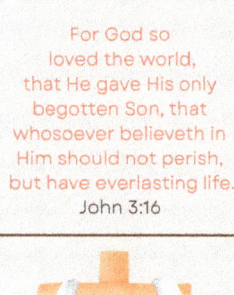

| | | |
|---|---|---|
| For God so loved the world, that He gave His only begotten Son, that whosoever believeth in Him should not perish, but have everlasting life. John 3:16 |  Holy Communion | Make a joyful noise unto the Lord, all the earth: make a loud noise, and rejoice, and sing praise. Psalm 98:4 |
|  | This is my **body** which is **given for you**: this do in remembrance of me. Luke 22:19<br><br>This cup is the New Testament in my **blood**, **which is shed for you**. Luke 22:20 |  |
| The Second Chapter of Acts |  | arise, and be baptized, and wash away thy sins, calling on the name of the Lord. Acts 22:16 |
|  | If ye then be risen with Christ, seek those things which are above, where Christ sitteth on the right hand of God. Colossians 3:1 |  |

MONTH

Cause me to hear thy lovingkindness in the morning; for in thee do I trust:   Psalm 143:8

54

The Lord is my shepherd; I shall not want.  He maketh me to lie down in green pastures: He leadeth me beside the still waters.   Psalm 23: 1-2

# TEA TIME

Take time to rest in His gentle loving-kindness. Slowly take a deep breath. As you exhale allow your muscles to relax and let go. Praise God. Thank you, my Lord, that I can leave all of my burdens and cares at Your feet. You are forever faithful. Please help me to keep You close to my heart, and always remember that I am a child of God and I walk in faith, not fear.

Now, have your favourite beverage, and enjoy the Word of God, slowly, carefully, and thoughtfully.

Spend some time this month in Colossians, Philippians and Ephesians or keep choosing scriptures from one of these pages, digging deeper, and exploring the surrounding scriptures.

## NOTES

_____

_____

_____

_____

_____

He restoreth my soul: He leadeth me in the paths of righteousness for His Name's sake.   Psalm 23:3

# The Goodness of God

## Noticing Goodness Every Day

Monday
------------------------------
------------------------------
------------------------------
------------------------------

Tuesday
------------------------------
------------------------------
------------------------------
------------------------------

Wednesday
------------------------------
------------------------------
------------------------------
------------------------------

Thursday
------------------------------
------------------------------
------------------------------
------------------------------

Friday
------------------------------
------------------------------
------------------------------
------------------------------

Saturday
------------------------------
------------------------------
------------------------------
------------------------------

Sunday
------------------------------
------------------------------
------------------------------
------------------------------

Because thy lovingkindness is better than life, my lips shall praise thee.   Psalm 63:3

# With a Grateful Heart

I have so many things in my life to be thankful for:

_____
_____
_____
_____
_____
_____
_____
_____
_____
_____
_____
_____

Rejoice evermore. Pray without ceasing. In everything give thanks: for this is the will of God in Christ Jesus concerning you.   1 Thessalonians 5:16-18

# It's time to pray

## New Prayer Requests

_____
_____
_____
_____
_____
_____
_____
_____
_____

## Answered Prayers

_____
_____
_____
_____
_____
_____
_____
_____
_____

## My Daily Prayers

_____
_____
_____
_____
_____
_____
_____
_____
_____
_____

Give ear to my words, O Lord, consider my meditation. Hearken unto the voice of my cry, my King, and my God: for unto thee will I pray.   Psalm 5:1-2

Fulfil ye my joy, that ye be likeminded, having the same love, being of one accord, of one mind. Let nothing be done through strife or vainglory; but in lowliness of mind let each esteem other better than themselves.   Philippians 2:2-3

# FIVE-MINUTE THOUGHTS

## ABOUT MY WALK

| FAVORITE SCRIPTURES | GREAT WORSHIP SONGS |
|---|---|
| · | · |
| · | · |
| · | · |

Look not every man on his own things, but every man also on the things of others.  Let this mind be in you, which was also in Christ Jesus:   Philippians 2:4-5

But are helpers of your joy: for by faith ye stand.
2 Corinthians 1:24

# FAITH
# *Builders*

I see the Lord moving in my life:

_____
_____
_____
_____
_____
_____
_____
_____
_____
_____
_____

Great is thy faithfulness.
Lamentations 3:23

# Draw

Draw nigh to God, and He will draw nigh to you.
James 4:8

But the wisdom that is from above is first pure, then peaceable, gentle, and easy to be entreated, full of mercy and good fruits, without partiality, and without hypocrisy. And the fruit of righteousness is sown in peace of them that make peace.
James 3:17-18

Consider: The wisdom of God is pure, peaceable, gentle, merciful, and easy to be entreated (being kind and reasonable toward one's request).

# THOUGHTS

# THOUGHTS

# THOUGHTS

Now faith is the substance of things hoped for, the evidence of things not seen.   Hebrews 11:1

# Faith in Action

| Helping | Practicing | Attending |
|---|---|---|
| Sharing | Praying | Giving |
| Tithing | Volunteering | Loving |

MONTH

for whatsoever a man soweth, that shall he also reap.   Galatians 6:7

To every thing there is a season, and a time to every purpose under the heaven:   Ecclesiastes 3:1

# TEA TIME

Take time to rest in His gentle loving-kindness. Slowly take a deep breath. As you exhale allow your muscles to relax and let go. Praise God. Thank you, my Lord, that I can leave all of my burdens and cares at Your feet. You are forever faithful. Please help me to keep You close to my heart and always remember that I am a child of God and I walk in faith, not fear.

Now, have your favourite beverage, and enjoy the Word of God, slowly, carefully, and thoughtfully.

Read Galatians, and Timothy 1 and 2, or choose a scripture from one of these pages, digging deeper, and exploring the surrounding scriptures.

### Notes

Every word of God is pure: He is a shield unto them that put their trust in Him.   Proverbs 30:5

# The Goodness of God

## Noticing Goodness Every Day

### Monday
------------------------------
------------------------------
------------------------------
------------------------------

### Tuesday
------------------------------
------------------------------
------------------------------
------------------------------

### Wednesday
------------------------------
------------------------------
------------------------------
------------------------------

### Thursday
------------------------------
------------------------------
------------------------------
------------------------------

### Friday
------------------------------
------------------------------
------------------------------
------------------------------

### Saturday
------------------------------
------------------------------
------------------------------
------------------------------

### Sunday
------------------------------
------------------------------
------------------------------
------------------------------

Surely goodness and mercy shall follow me all the days of my life: and I will dwell in the House of the Lord for ever.   Psalm 23:6

# With a Grateful Heart

I have so many things in my life to be thankful for:

Oh give thanks unto the Lord; for He is good; for His mercy endureth for ever.   1 Chronicles 16:34

# It's time to pray

## New Prayer Requests

## Answered Prayers

## My Daily Prayers

My voice shalt thou hear in the morning, O Lord; in the morning will I direct my prayer unto thee, and will look up.   Psalm 5:3

The Lord is on my side; I will not fear:
what can man do unto me?   Psalm 118:6

# FIVE-MINUTE THOUGHTS
## ABOUT MY WALK

| FAVOURITE SCRIPTURES | GREAT WORSHIP SONGS |
|---|---|
| • | • |
| • | • |
| • | • |
| • | • |

And the very God of peace sanctify you wholly; and I pray
God your whole spirit and soul and body be preserved
blameless unto the coming of our Lord Jesus Christ.
1 Thessalonians 5:23

> For whatsoever is born of God overcometh the world; and this is the victory that overcometh the world, even our faith.   1 John 5:4

## FAITH *Builders*

I see the Lord moving in my life:

___

___

___

___

___

___

___

___

___

___

___

___

___

> But these are written, that ye might believe that Jesus is the Christ, the Son of God; and that believing ye might have life through His Name.   John 20:31

# Believe

But without faith it is impossible to please Him: for he that cometh to God must believe that He is, and that He is a rewarder of them that diligently seek Him.   Hebrews 11:6

Let not your heart be troubled: ye believe in God, believe also in me. In my Father's house are many mansions: if it were not so, I would have told you. I go to prepare a place for you. And if I go and prepare a place for you, I will come again, and receive you unto myself; that where I am, there ye may be also.  John 14:1-3

Consider:  I go to prepare a place for you.

# THOUGHTS

# THOUGHTS

# THOUGHTS

And He said unto them, Go ye into all the world, and preach the Gospel to every creature.   Mark 16:15

# Share the
# LOVE of JESUS

MONTH

How beautiful are the feet of them that preach the gospel of peace, and bring glad tidings of good things!   Romans 10:15

Blessed be God, even the Father of our Lord Jesus Christ, the Father of mercies, and the God of all comfort; 2 Corinthians 1:3

# TEA TIME

Take time to rest in His gentle loving-kindness. Slowly take a deep breath. As you exhale allow your muscles to relax and let go. Praise God. Thank you, my Lord, that I can leave all of my burdens and cares at Your feet. You are forever faithful. Please help me to keep You close to my heart and always remember that I am a child of God and I walk in faith, not fear.

Now, have your favourite beverage, and enjoy the Word of God, slowly, carefully, and thoughtfully.

Spend time this month in Psalms and Proverbs in the Old Testament. They are filled with emotion, wisdom, and love.

## NOTES

_____
_____
_____
_____
_____

Glory ye in His holy Name: let the heart of them rejoice that seek the Lord.
1 Chronicles 16:10

# The Goodness of God

## Noticing Goodness Every Day

Monday
--------------------
--------------------
--------------------
--------------------

Tuesday
--------------------
--------------------
--------------------
--------------------

Wednesday
--------------------
--------------------
--------------------
--------------------

Thursday
--------------------
--------------------
--------------------
--------------------

Friday
--------------------
--------------------
--------------------
--------------------

Saturday
--------------------
--------------------
--------------------
--------------------

Sunday
--------------------
--------------------
--------------------
--------------------

And now, Lord, thou art God, and hast promised this goodness unto thy servant. 1 Chronicles 17:26

# With a Grateful Heart

I have so many things in my life to be thankful for:

_____
_____
_____
_____
_____
_____
_____
_____
_____
_____
_____
_____
_____
_____
_____
_____

But the Lord is faithful, who shall stablish you, and keep you from evil.  2 Thessalonians 3:3

## It's time to pray

### New Prayer Requests

### Answered Prayers

### My Daily Prayers

And God is able to make all grace abound toward you; that ye, always having all sufficiency in all things, may abound to every good work:
2 Corinthians 9:8

Moreover whom He did predestinate, them He also called: and whom He called, them He also justified: and whom He justified, them He also glorified. What shall we then say to these things? If God be for us, who can be against us?
Romans 8:30-31

# FIVE-MINUTE THOUGHTS

## ABOUT MY WALK

| FAVOURITE SCRIPTURES | GREAT WORSHIP SONGS |
|---|---|
| · | · |
| · | · |
| · | · |
| · | · |

He that spared not His own Son, but delivered Him up for us all, how shall He not with Him also freely give us all things?   Romans 8:32

He shall not be afraid of evil tidings: his heart is fixed, trusting in the Lord.   Psalm 112:7

# FAITH
## *Builders*

I see the Lord moving in my life:

_____
_____
_____
_____
_____
_____
_____
_____
_____
_____
_____

Looking for that blessed hope, and glorious appearing of the great God and our Saviour Jesus Christ; Who gave Himself for us, that He might redeem us from all iniquity, and purify unto Himself a peculiar people, zealous of good works.   Titus 2:13-14

# Inspiration

All scripture is given by inspiration of God, and is profitable for doctrine, for reproof, for correction, for instruction in righteousness:  2 Timothy 3:16

But as it is written, Eye hath not seen, nor ear heard, neither have entered into the heart of man, the things which God hath prepared for them that love Him.
1 Corinthians 2:9

Consider:  The things which God hath prepared for them that love Him.

# THOUGHTS

# THOUGHTS

# THOUGHTS

And let us consider one another to provoke unto love and to good works: Not forsaking the assembling of ourselves together, as the manner of some is; but exhorting one another: and so much the more, as ye see the day approaching.   Hebrews 10:24-25

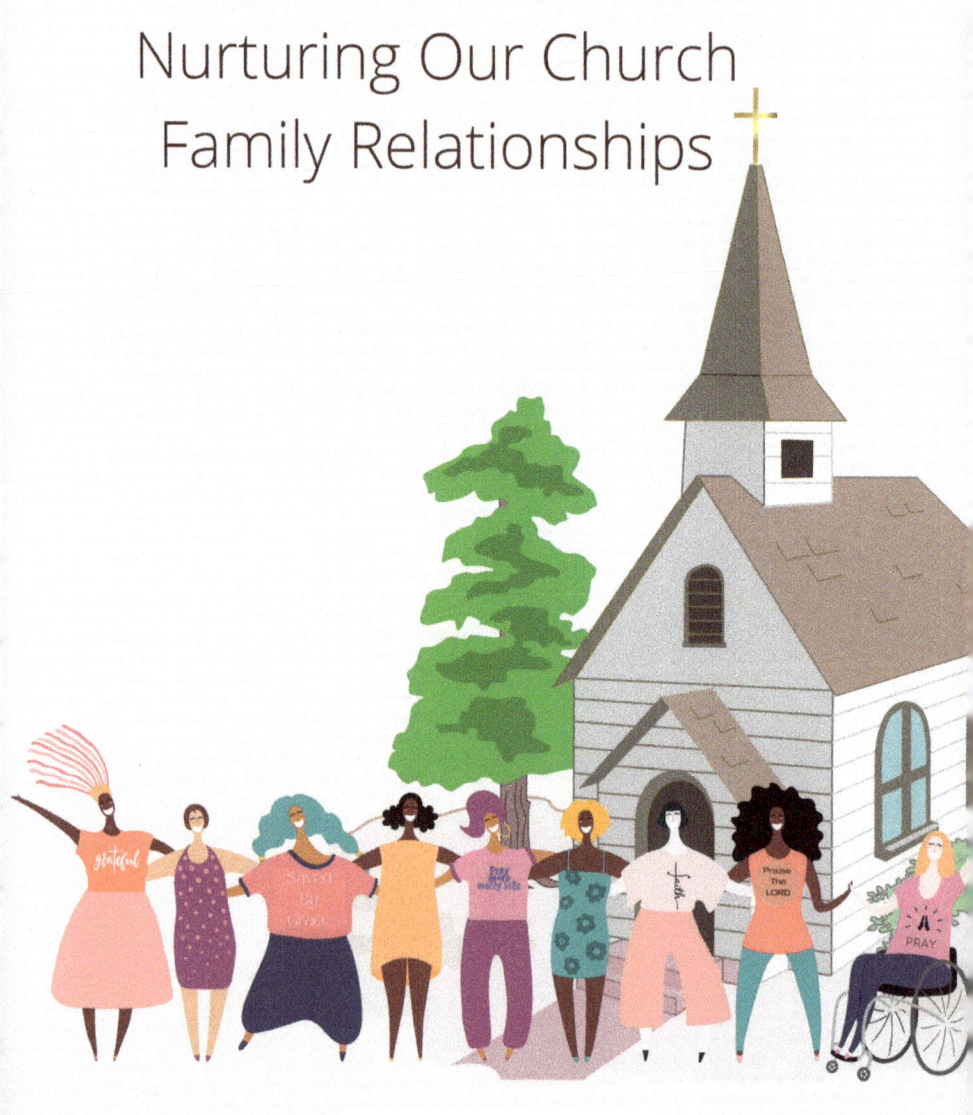

# Nurturing Our Church Family Relationships

MONTH

Wherefore comfort yourselves together, and edify one another, even as also ye do.  1 Thessalonians 5:11

That the God of our Lord Jesus Christ, the Father of glory, may give unto you the spirit of wisdom and revelation in the knowledge of Him:   Ephesians 1:17

# TEA TIME

Take time to rest in His gentle loving-kindness. Slowly take a deep breath. As you exhale allow your muscles to relax and let go. Praise God. Thank you, my Lord, that I can leave all of my burdens and cares at Your feet. You are forever faithful. Please help me to keep You close to my heart and always remember that I am a child of God and I walk in faith, not fear.

Now, have your favourite beverage, and enjoy the Word of God, slowly, carefully, and thoughtfully.

Back in the New Testament read Romans, focus on Romans 8, living life in the Spirit, it is life changing. Or continue to explore the scriptures.

## NOTES

_____

_____

_____

_____

_____

_____

The eyes of your understanding being enlightened; that ye may know what is the hope of His calling, and what the riches of the glory of His inheritance in the saints,   Ephesians 1:18

# The Goodness of God

## Noticing Goodness Every Day

**Monday**
----------------
----------------
----------------

**Tuesday**
----------------
----------------
----------------

**Wednesday**
----------------
----------------
----------------

**Thursday**
----------------
----------------
----------------

**Friday**
----------------
----------------
----------------

**Saturday**
----------------
----------------
----------------

**Sunday**
----------------
----------------
----------------

*That the name of our Lord Jesus Christ may be glorified in you, and ye in Him, according to the grace of our God and the Lord Jesus Christ.* 2 Thessalonians 1:12

# With a Grateful Heart

I have so many things in my life to be thankful for:

_____

_____

_____

_____

_____

_____

_____

_____

_____

*For God hath not given us the spirit of fear; but of power, and of love, and of a sound mind.*
2 Timothy 1:7

# It's time to pray

## New Prayer Requests

_____
_____
_____
_____
_____
_____
_____
_____
_____

## Answered Prayers

_____
_____
_____
_____
_____
_____
_____
_____
_____

## My Daily Prayers

_____
_____
_____
_____
_____
_____
_____
_____
_____

Hear me, O Lord; for thy lovingkindness is good: turn unto me according to the multitude of thy tender mercies. Psalm 69:16

Trust in the Lord with all thine heart; and lean not unto thine own understanding. In all thy ways acknowledge Him, and He shall direct thy paths.   Proverbs 3:5-6

# FIVE-MINUTE THOUGHTS

## ABOUT MY WALK

| FAVOURITE SCRIPTURES | GREAT WORSHIP SONGS |
|---|---|
| • | • |
| • | • |
| • | • |
| • | • |

I am crucified with Christ: nevertheless I live; yet not I, but Christ liveth in me: and the life which I now live in the flesh I live by the faith of the Son of God, who loved me, and gave Himself for me.   Galatians 2:20

Jesus said unto him, If thou canst believe, all things are possible to him that believeth.
Mark 9:23

# FAITH
*Builders*

I see the Lord moving in my life:

_____
_____
_____
_____
_____
_____
_____
_____
_____
_____
_____

Verily, verily, I say unto you, He that heareth my Word, and believeth on Him that sent me, hath everlasting life, and shall not come into condemnation; but is passed from death unto life.
John 5:24

# Rejoice

> But let the righteous be glad: let them rejoice before God: yea, let them exceedingly rejoice.
> Psalm 68:3

Blessed be the God and Father of our Lord Jesus Christ, which according to His abundant mercy hath begotten us again unto a lively hope by the resurrection of Jesus Christ from the dead, to an inheritance incorruptible, and undefiled, and that fadeth not away, reserved in heaven for you,
1 Peter 1:3-4

Consider: A lively hope, also an inheritance reserved in heaven, just for you.

# THOUGHTS

# THOUGHTS

# THOUGHTS

# Put on the whole armour of God

Be strong in the Lord and in the power of His might.   Ephesians 6:10

| The breastplate of righteousness | The helmet of Salvation | Loins girt about with truth |
|---|---|---|
| Feet shod with the preparation of the Gospel of peace | The shield of faith | The sword of the Spirit, which is the Word of God: |

Put on the whole armour of God, that ye may be able to stand against the wiles of the devil. For we wrestle not against flesh and blood but against principalities against powers, against the rulers of the darkness of this world, against spiritual wickedness in high places.   Ephesians 6:11-12

For I the Lord thy God will hold thy right hand,
saying unto thee, Fear not; I will help thee.
Isaiah:41:13

# TEA TIME

Take time to rest in His gentle loving-kindness. Slowly take a deep breath. As you exhale allow your muscles to relax and let go. Praise God. Thank you, my Lord, that I can leave all of my burdens and cares at Your feet. You are forever faithful. Please help me to keep You close to my heart and always remember that I am a child of God and I walk in faith, not fear.

Now, have your favourite beverage, and enjoy the Word of God, slowly, carefully, and thoughtfully.

Read Titus, Philemon, James, Peter 1 and 2 and Jude, or continue explore the scriptures.

### NOTES

_____

_____

_____

_____

_____

Be strong and of good courage, fear not, nor be afraid of them: for the Lord thy God, He it is that doth go with thee; He will not fail thee nor forsake thee.   Deuteronomy 31:6

# The Goodness of God

## Noticing Goodness Every Day

Monday

------------------------------------
------------------------------------
------------------------------------
------------------------------------

Tuesday

------------------------------------
------------------------------------
------------------------------------
------------------------------------

Wednesday

------------------------------------
------------------------------------
------------------------------------
------------------------------------

Thursday

------------------------------------
------------------------------------
------------------------------------
------------------------------------

Friday

------------------------------------
------------------------------------
------------------------------------
------------------------------------

Saturday

------------------------------------
------------------------------------
------------------------------------
------------------------------------

Sunday

------------------------------------
------------------------------------
------------------------------------
------------------------------------

Greater is He that is in you, than he that is in the world.   1 John 4:4

# With a Grateful Heart

**I have so many things in my life to be thankful for:**

_____
_____
_____
_____
_____
_____
_____
_____
_____
_____
_____
_____

I am Alpha and Omega, the beginning and
the ending, saith the Lord, which is, and was,
and which is to come, the Almighty.
Revelation 1:8

# It's time to pray

## New Prayer Requests

## Answered Prayers

## My Daily Prayers

Wherefore also we pray always for you, that our God would count you worthy of this calling, and fulfil all the good pleasure of His goodness, and the work of faith with power. 2 Thessalonians 1:11

Every good gift and every perfect gift is from above, and cometh down from the Father of lights, with whom is no variableness, neither shadow of turning.   James 1:17

# FIVE-MINUTE THOUGHTS

## ABOUT MY WALK

**FAVOURITE SCRIPTURES**
·
·
·
·

**GREAT WORSHIP SONGS**
·
·
·
·

Behold, I stand at the door, and knock: if any man hear my voice, and open the door, I will come in to him, and will sup with him, and he with me.
Revelation 3:20

That Christ may dwell in your hearts by faith; that ye being rooted and grounded in love, May be able to comprehend with all saints what is the breadth, and length, and depth, and height;   Ephesians 3:17-18

# FAITH *Builders*

I see the Lord moving in my life:

_____
_____
_____
_____
_____
_____
_____
_____
_____
_____
_____

And to know the love of Christ, which passeth knowledge, that ye might be filled with all the fullness of God.
Ephesians 3:19

# Ponder

Ponder the path of thy feet, and let all thy ways be established.  Proverbs 4:26

That the trial of your faith, being much more precious than of gold that perisheth, though it be tried with fire, might be found unto praise and honour and glory at the appearing of Jesus Christ: Whom having not seen, ye love; in whom, though now ye see Him not, yet believing, ye rejoice with joy unspeakable and full of glory: Recieving the end of your faith, even the salvation of your souls.   1 Peter 1:7-9

Consider: Our trails are much more precious

than gold the perishes.  They build faith.

# THOUGHTS

# THOUGHTS

# THOUGHTS

According as He hath chosen us in Him before the foundation of the world, that we should be holy and without blame before Him in love: Having predestinated us unto the adoption of children by Jesus Christ to Himself, according to the good pleasure of His will.   Ephesians 1:4-5

## Before the foundation of the world

To the praise of the glory of His grace, wherein He hath made us accepted in the beloved.   Ephesians 1:6

Therefore being justified by faith, we have peace with God through our Lord Jesus Christ: by whom also we have access by faith into this grace wherein we stand, and rejoice in hope of the glory of God.   Romans 5:1-2

# TEA TIME

Take time to rest in His gentle loving-kindness. Slowly take a deep breath. As you exhale allow your muscles to relax and let go. Praise God. Thank you, my Lord, that I can leave all of my burdens and cares at Your feet. You are forever faithful. Please help me to keep You close to my heart and always remember that I am a child of God and I walk in faith, not fear.

Now, have your favourite beverage, and enjoy the Word of God, slowly, carefully, and thoughtfully.

Spend some time in Acts, our God is our miracle worker or continue to explore the scriptures.

### NOTES

---

---

---

---

---

The Lord thy God in the midst of the is mighty; He will save, He will rejoice over thee with joy; He will rest in His love, He will joy over thee with singing.   Zephaniah 3:17

# The Goodness of God

## Noticing Goodness Every Day

Monday
------------------------------
------------------------------
------------------------------

Tuesday
------------------------------
------------------------------
------------------------------

Wednesday
------------------------------
------------------------------
------------------------------

Thursday
------------------------------
------------------------------
------------------------------

Friday
------------------------------
------------------------------
------------------------------

Saturday
------------------------------
------------------------------
------------------------------

Sunday
------------------------------
------------------------------
------------------------------

My goodness, and my fortress; my high tower, and my deliverer; my shield, and He in whom I trust;
Psalm 144:2

# With a Grateful Heart

I have so many things in my life to be thankful for:

_____
_____
_____
_____
_____
_____
_____
_____
_____
_____
_____

Now we have received, not the spirit of the world, but the spirit which is of God; that we might know the things that are freely given to us of God.  1 Corinthians 2:12

# *It's time to pray*

## New Prayer Requests

## Answered Prayers

## My Daily Prayers

Fight the good fight of faith, lay hold on eternal life, whereunto thou art also called, and hast professed a good profession before many witnesses. 1 Timothy 6:12

Now therefore ye are no more strangers and foreigners, but fellowcitizens with the saints, and of the household of God: and are built upon the foundation of the apostles and prophets, Jesus Christ being the chief cornerstone;  Ephesians 2:19-20

# FIVE-MINUTE THOUGHTS

## ABOUT MY WALK

| FAVOURITE SCRIPTURES | GREAT WORSHIP SONGS |
| --- | --- |
| • | • |
| • | • |
| • | • |
| • | • |

Praise the Lord; for the Lord is good: sing praises unto His name; for it is pleasant.  Psalm 135:3

*If ye abide in me, and my words abide in you, ye shall ask what ye will, and it shall be done unto you.  John 15:7*

# FAITH
## *Builders*

I see the Lord moving in my life:

_____
_____
_____
_____
_____
_____
_____
_____
_____
_____
_____

*That the communication of thy faith may become effectual by the acknowledging of every good thing which is in you in Christ Jesus.  Philemon 1:6*

# Glory

Glory ye in His holy Name:  Let the heart of them rejoice that seek the Lord.   Psalm 105:3

Now the God of peace, that brought again from the dead our Lord Jesus, that great shepherd of the sheep, through the blood of the everlasting covenant, make you perfect in every good work to do His will, working in you that which is well pleasing in His sight, through Jesus Christ; to whom be glory for ever and ever. Amen.   Hebrews 13:20

Consider: Make you perfect in every good work.

# THOUGHTS

# THOUGHTS

# THOUGHTS

# The beauty of God's Creation

MONTH

For thus saith the Lord that created the heavens; God Himself that formed the earth and made it; He hath established it, He created it not in vain, He formed it to be inhabited: I am the Lord; and there is none else.   Isaiah 45:18

126

Those things, which ye have both learned, and received, and heard, and seen in me, do: and the God of peace shall be with you.   Philippians 4:9

# TEA TIME

Take time to rest in His gentle loving-kindness. Slowly take a deep breath. As you exhale allow your muscles to relax and let go. Praise God. Thank you, my Lord, that I can leave all of my burdens and cares at Your feet. You are forever faithful. Please help me to keep You close to my heart and always remember that I am a child of God and I walk in faith, not fear.

Now, have your favourite beverage, and enjoy the Word of God, slowly, carefully, and thoughtfully.

Spend time in Corinthians 1 and 2 this month or continue to explore the scriptures.

### NOTES

_____
_____
_____
_____
_____
_____

For in Him dwelleth all the fulness of the Godhead bodily.  And ye are complete in Him, which is the head of all principality and power:  Colossians 2:9-10

# The Goodness of God

## Noticing Goodness Every Day

| Monday | Tuesday |
|---|---|
| ............................................. | ............................................. |
| ............................................. | ............................................. |
| ............................................. | ............................................. |
| ............................................. | ............................................. |

| Wednesday | Thursday |
|---|---|
| ............................................. | ............................................. |
| ............................................. | ............................................. |
| ............................................. | ............................................. |
| ............................................. | ............................................. |

| Friday | Saturday |
|---|---|
| ............................................. | ............................................. |
| ............................................. | ............................................. |
| ............................................. | ............................................. |
| ............................................. | ............................................. |

| Sunday | |
|---|---|
| ............................................. | ............................................. |
| ............................................. | ............................................. |
| ............................................. | ............................................. |
| ............................................. | ............................................. |

My goodness, and my fortress; my high tower, and my deliverer; my shield, and He in whom I trust;
Psalm 144:2

# With a Grateful Heart

I have so many things in my life to be thankful for:

_____
_____
_____
_____
_____
_____
_____
_____
_____
_____
_____

And the Lord passed by before him, and proclaimed, The Lord the Lord God, merciful and gracious, longsuffering, and abundant in goodness and truth.   Exodus 34:6

# It's time to pray

### New Prayer Requests

### Answered Prayers

### My Daily Prayers

Continue in prayer, and watch in the same with thanksgiving, withal praying also for us, that God would open unto us a door of utterance, to speak the mystery of Christ,   Colossians 2:2-3

That ye might walk worthy of the Lord unto all pleasing, being fruitful in every good work, and increasing in the knowledge of God;   Colossians 1:10

# FIVE-MINUTE THOUGHTS

## ABOUT MY WALK

| FAVOURITE SCRIPTURES | GREAT WORSHIP SONGS |
|---|---|
| • | • |
| • | • |
| • | • |
| • | • |

But my God shall supply all your need according to His riches in glory by Christ Jesus. Philippians 4:19

O love the Lord, all ye His saints: the Lord preserveth the faithful, and plenitfully rewardeth the proud doer.   Psalm 31:23

# FAITH
## *Builders*

I see the Lord moving in my life:

_____
_____
_____
_____
_____
_____
_____
_____
_____
_____
_____

But when Jesus heard it, He answered him, saying: Fear not: Believe only, and she shall be made whole.
Luke 8:50

# Hope

And hope maketh not ashamed; because the love of God is shed abroad in our hearts by the Holy Ghost which is given unto us.   Romans 5:5

Though I speak with the tongues of men and of angels, and have not charity, I am become as sounding brass, or a tinkling cymbal. And though I have the gift of prophecy, and understand all mysteries, and all knowledge; and though I have all faith, so that I could remove mountains, and have not charity, I am nothing.  1 Corinthians 13:1-2

Consider:  Charity = Love

# THOUGHTS

# THOUGHTS

# THOUGHTS

## And He opened His mouth and taught them, saying

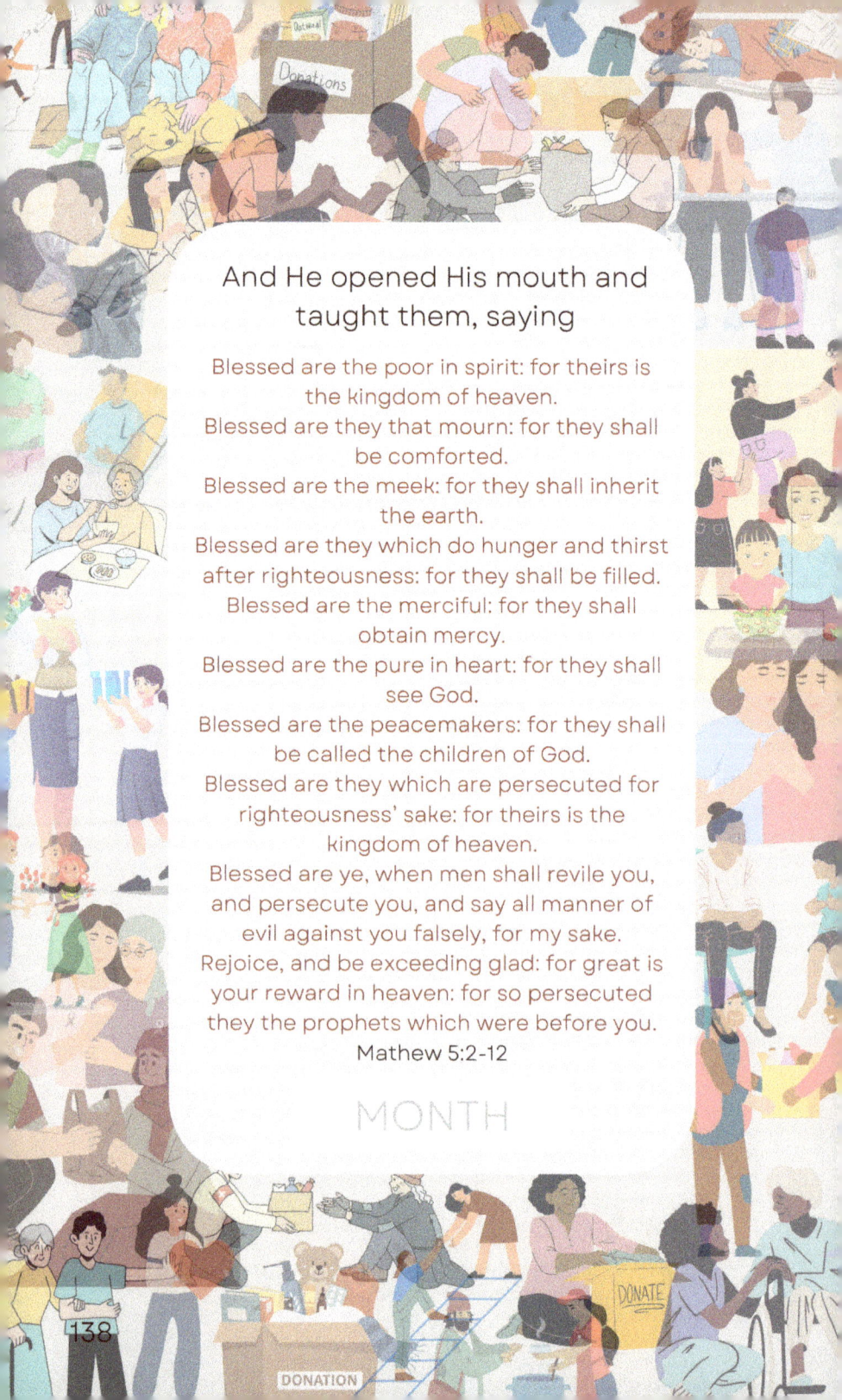

Blessed are the poor in spirit: for theirs is the kingdom of heaven.
Blessed are they that mourn: for they shall be comforted.
Blessed are the meek: for they shall inherit the earth.
Blessed are they which do hunger and thirst after righteousness: for they shall be filled.
Blessed are the merciful: for they shall obtain mercy.
Blessed are the pure in heart: for they shall see God.
Blessed are the peacemakers: for they shall be called the children of God.
Blessed are they which are persecuted for righteousness' sake: for theirs is the kingdom of heaven.
Blessed are ye, when men shall revile you, and persecute you, and say all manner of evil against you falsely, for my sake.
Rejoice, and be exceeding glad: for great is your reward in heaven: for so persecuted they the prophets which were before you.

Mathew 5:2-12

MONTH

There remaineth therefore a rest to the people of God.   Hebrews 4:9

---

# TEA TIME

Take time to rest in His gentle loving-kindness. Slowly take a deep breath. As you exhale allow your muscles to relax and let go. Praise God. Thank you, my Lord, that I can leave all of my burdens and cares at Your feet. You are forever faithful. Please help me to keep You close to my heart and always remember that I am a child of God and I walk in faith, not fear.

Now, have your favourite beverage, and enjoy the Word of God, slowly, carefully, and thoughtfully.

-Read Hebrews and also go back and read the words of Jesus in red, full of love, comfort and wisdom or continue to explore the scriptures

### NOTES

_____

_____

_____

_____

_____

_____

For though I be absent in the flesh, yet am I with you in the Spirit, joying and beholding your order, and the stedfastness of your faith in Christ.   Colossians 2:5

# The Goodness of God

## Noticing Goodness Every Day

Monday

Tuesday

Wednesday

Thursday

Friday

Saturday

Sunday

O give thanks unto the Lord; for He is good: for His mercy endureth for ever.   Psalm 106:1

# With a Grateful Heart

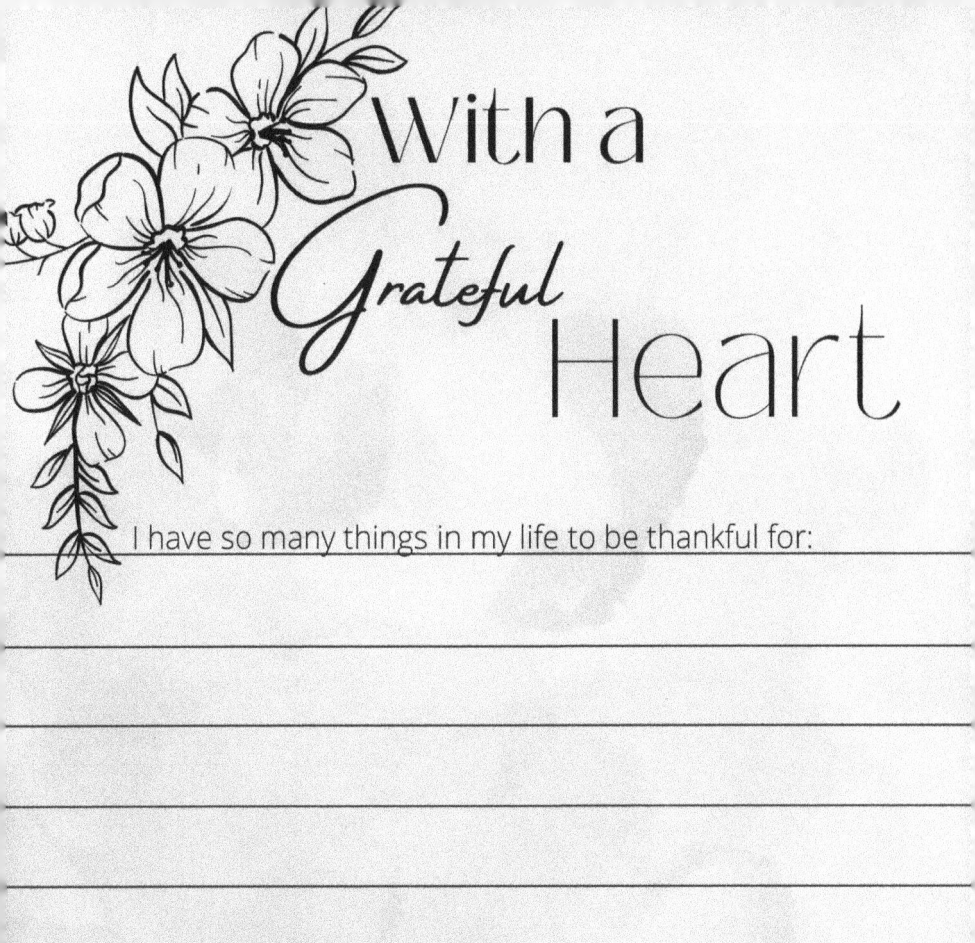

I have so many things in my life to be thankful for:

For this cause also thank we God without ceasing, because, when ye received the Word of God which ye heard of us, ye received it not as the word of men, but as it is in truth, the Word of God, which effectually worketh also in you that believe. 1 Thessalonians 2:13

# It's time to pray

## New Prayer Requests

_____
_____
_____
_____
_____
_____
_____
_____

## Answered Prayers

_____
_____
_____
_____
_____
_____
_____
_____

## My Daily Prayers

_____
_____
_____
_____
_____
_____
_____
_____
_____
_____

Confess your faults one to another, and pray one for another, that ye may be healed. The effectual fervent prayer of a righteous man availeth much.
James 5:17

Be of good courage, and He shall strengthen
your heart, all ye that hope in the Lord.
Psalm 31:24

# FIVE-MINUTE THOUGHTS

## ABOUT MY WALK

| FAVOURITE SCRIPTURES | GREAT WORSHIP SONGS |
|---|---|
| • | • |
| • | • |
| • | • |
| • | • |

The Lord is my rock, and my fortress, and my deliverer;
my God, my strength, in whom I will trust; my buckler,
and the horn of my Salvation, and my high tower.
Psalm 18:2

There hath no temptation taken you but such as is common to man: but God is faithful, who will not suffer you to be tempted above that ye are able; but will with the temptation also make a way to escape, that ye may be able to bear it.  1 Corinthians 10:13

# FAITH Builders

I see the Lord moving in my life:

_____
_____
_____
_____
_____
_____
_____
_____
_____
_____
_____

For unto us was the gospel preached, as well as unto them: but the word preached did not profit them, not being mixed with faith in them that heard it.  Hebrews 4:2

# Truth

Oh Lord, thou art my God; I will exalt thee, I will praise thy name for thou hast done wonderful things; thy counsels of old are faithfulness and truth.   Isaiah 25:1

Nay, in all these things we are more than conquerors through Him that loved us. For I am persuaded, that neither death, nor life, nor angels, nor principalities, nor powers, nor things present, nor things to come, shall be able to separate us from the love of God, which is in Christ Jesus our Lord.   Romans 8:37-39

Consider:  We are more than conquerors

# THOUGHTS

# THOUGHTS

# THOUGHTS

# Abundant Life

But after that the kindness and love of God our Saviour toward man appeared, Not by works of righteousness which we have done, but according to His mercy He saved us, by the washing of regeneration, and renewing of the Holy Ghost; Which He shed on us abundantly through Jesus Christ our Saviour; That being justified by His grace, we should be made heirs according to the hope of eternal life.   Titus 3:4-7

MONTH

Let your conversations be without covetousness; and be content with such things as ye have: for He hath said, I will never leave thee nor forsake thee.   Hebrews 13:5

*Wisdom is the principal thing; therefore get wisdom: and with all thy getting get understanding.   Proverbs 4:7*

# TEA TIME

Take time to rest in His gentle loving-kindness. Slowly take a deep breath. As you exhale allow your muscles to relax and let go. Praise God. Thank you, my Lord, that I can leave all of my burdens and cares at Your feet. You are forever faithful. Please help me to keep You close to my heart and always remember that I am a child of God and I walk in faith, not fear.

Now, have your favourite beverage, and enjoy the Word of God, slowly, carefully, and thoughtfully.

It's time for Revelation or continue to explore the scriptures.

NOTES

_____

_____

_____

_____

_____

_____

*For wisdom is better than rubies; and all the things that may be desired are not to be compared to it.   Proverbs 8:11*

# The Goodness of God

## Noticing Goodness Every Day

### Monday
------------------------------
------------------------------
------------------------------
------------------------------

### Tuesday
------------------------------
------------------------------
------------------------------
------------------------------

### Wednesday
------------------------------
------------------------------
------------------------------
------------------------------

### Thursday
------------------------------
------------------------------
------------------------------
------------------------------

### Friday
------------------------------
------------------------------
------------------------------
------------------------------

### Saturday
------------------------------
------------------------------
------------------------------
------------------------------

### Sunday
------------------------------
------------------------------
------------------------------
------------------------------

*For how great is His goodness, and how great is His beauty! Zechariah 9:17*

# With a Grateful Heart

I have so many things in my life to be thankful for:

_____
_____
_____
_____
_____
_____
_____
_____
_____
_____
_____
_____
_____

And to stand every morning to thank and praise the Lord, and likewise at even; 1 Chronicles 23:30

# It's time to pray

## New Prayer Requests

_____
_____
_____
_____
_____
_____
_____
_____

## Answered Prayers

_____
_____
_____
_____
_____
_____
_____
_____

## My Daily Prayers

_____
_____
_____
_____
_____
_____
_____
_____
_____
_____

Wait on the Lord: be of good courage, and He shall strengthen thine heart: wait, I say, on the Lord.
Psalm 27:14

But godliness with contentment is great gain.
1 Timothy 6:6

# FIVE-MINUTE THOUGHTS

## ABOUT MY WALK

FAVOURITE SCRIPTURES

- 
- 
- 

GREAT WORSHIP SONGS

- 
- 
- 

But whosoever drinketh of the water that I shall give him shall never thirst; but the water that I shall give him shall be in him a well of water springing up into everlasting life. John 4:14

The Lord bless thee, and keep thee: The Lord make His face shine upon thee, and be gracious unto thee: The Lord lift up His countenance upon thee, and give thee peace.   Numbers 6:24-26

# FAITH *Builders*

I see the Lord moving in my life:

_____
_____
_____
_____
_____
_____
_____
_____
_____
_____
_____
_____
_____

These things I have spoken unto you, that in me ye might have peace.  In the world ye shall have tribulation: but be of good cheer; I have overcome the world.   John 16:33

# Balance

Let me be weighted in an even balance that God may know mine integrity.   Job 31:6

Put on therefore, as the elect of God, holy and beloved, bowels of mercies, kindness, humbleness of mind, meekness, longsuffering; Forbearing one another, and forgiving one another, if any man have a quarrel against any: even as Christ forgave you, so also do ye. And above all these things put on charity, which is the bond of perfectness. And let the peace of God rule in your hearts, to the which also ye are called in one body; and be ye thankful.
Colossians 3:12-15

**Consider: Every word**

# THOUGHTS

# THOUGHTS

# THOUGHTS

# Virtues of living in the truth

According as His divine power hath given unto us all things that pertain unto life and godliness, through the knowledge of Him that hath called us to glory and virtue: Whereby are given unto us exceeding great and precious promises: that by these ye might be partakers of the divine nature, having escaped the corruption that is in the world through lust.   2 Peter 1:3-4

| Living a life of goodness | Freedom from guilt and shame | Comfort in the depths of your soul |
|---|---|---|
| Peace of mind | Deep spiritual Joy | A heart to Love |
| A clear conscience | Healthy mind healthy body | Emotionally free from anxiety and stress |

MONTH

He that followeth after righteousness and mercy findeth life, righteousness, and honour.   Proverbs 21:21

But the God of all grace, who hath called us unto His eternal glory by Christ Jesus, after that ye have suffered a while, make you perfect, stablish, strengthen, settle you. To Him be glory and dominion for ever and ever. Amen   1 Peter 5:10-11

# TEA TIME

Take time to rest in His gentle loving-kindness. Slowly take a deep breath. As you exhale allow your muscles to relax and let go. Praise God. Thank you, my Lord, that I can leave all of my burdens and cares at Your feet. You are forever faithful. Please help me to keep You close to my heart and always remember that I am a child of God and I walk in faith, not fear.

Now, have your favourite beverage, and enjoy the Word of God, slowly, carefully, and thoughtfully.

If you would like to read the Old Testament from beginning to end, read 2-3 chapters per day and you will finish it in about a year or continue to explore the scriptures.

NOTES

_____
_____
_____
_____
_____
_____

Casting all your care upon Him: for He careth for you.   1 Peter 5:7

# The Goodness of God

## Noticing Goodness Every Day

Monday
------------------------------
------------------------------
------------------------------
------------------------------

Tuesday
------------------------------
------------------------------
------------------------------
------------------------------

Wednesday
------------------------------
------------------------------
------------------------------
------------------------------

Thursday
------------------------------
------------------------------
------------------------------
------------------------------

Friday
------------------------------
------------------------------
------------------------------
------------------------------

Saturday
------------------------------
------------------------------
------------------------------
------------------------------

Sunday
------------------------------
------------------------------
------------------------------
------------------------------

Be not overcome of evil, but overcome evil with good.   Romans 12:21

# With a Grateful Heart

I have so many things in my life to be thankful for:

_____
_____
_____
_____
_____
_____
_____
_____
_____
_____
_____
_____

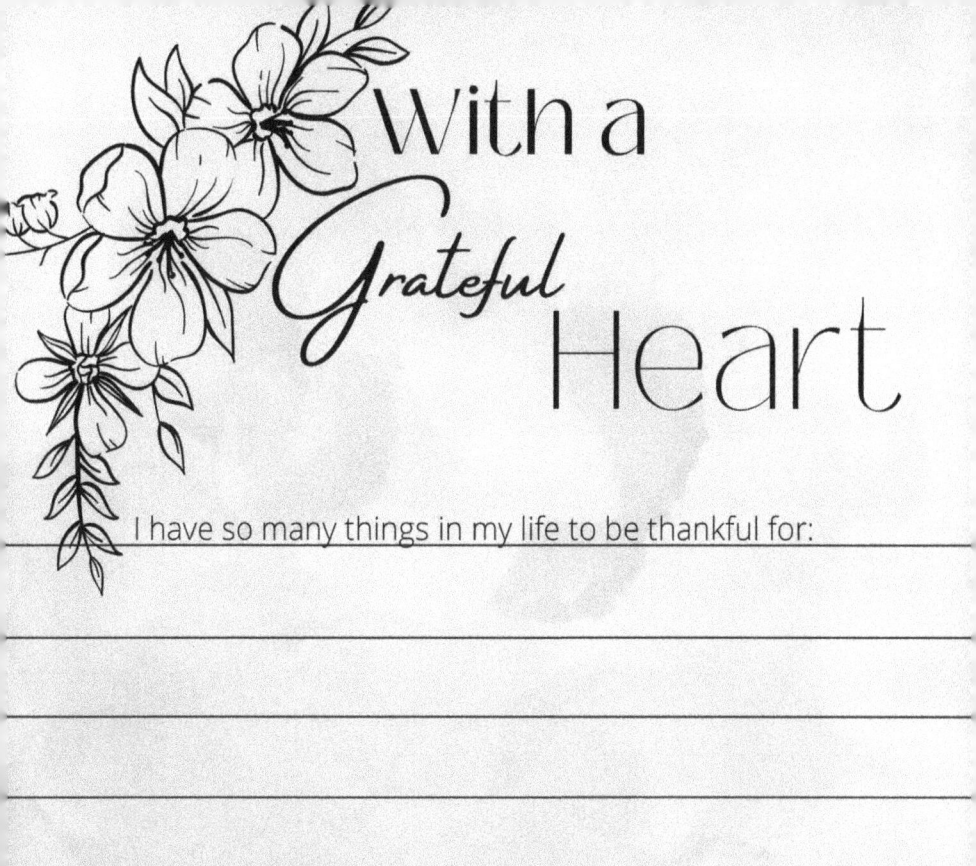

Speaking to yourselves in psalms and hymns and spiritual songs, singing and making melody in your heart to the Lord; Giving thanks always for all things unto God and the Father in the name of our Lord Jesus Christ;   Ephesians 5:19-20

# It's time to pray

## New Prayer Requests

## Answered Prayers

## My Daily Prayers

And this is the confidence that we have in Him, that, if we ask any thing according to His will, He heareth us: And if we know that He hear us, whatsoever we ask, we know that we have the petitions that we desired of Him. 1 John 5:14-15

But if we walk in the light, as He is in the light, we have fellowship one with another, and the blood of Jesus Christ His Son cleanseth us from all sin.  1 John 1:7

# FIVE-MINUTE THOUGHTS

## ABOUT MY WALK

_____
_____
_____
_____
_____
_____
_____
_____
_____
_____

| FAVOURITE SCRIPTURES | GREAT WORSHIP SONGS |
|---|---|
| • | • |
| • | • |
| • | • |
| • | • |

Then spake Jesus again unto them, saying, I am the light of the world: he that followeth me shall not walk in darkness, but shall have the light of life.  John 8:12

And we have known and believed the love that God hath to us. God is love; and he that dwelleth in love dwelleth in God, and God in him. 1 John 4:16

# FAITH *Builders*

I see the Lord moving in my life:

_____
_____
_____
_____
_____
_____
_____
_____
_____
_____
_____
_____

Herein is our love made perfect, that we may have boldness in the day of judgement: because as He is, so are we in this world. There is no fear in love; but perfect love casteth out fear: 1 John 4:17-18

# Abundance

But the meek shall inherit the earth; and shall delight themselves in the abundance of peace.
Psalm 37:11

For the Lord Himself shall descend from heaven with a shout, with the voice of the archangel, and with the trump of God: and the dead in Christ shall rise first: Then we which are alive and remain shall be caught up together with them in the clouds, to meet the Lord in the air: and so shall we ever be with the Lord. Wherefore comfort one another with these words.   1 Thessalonians 4:16-18

Consider: To meet the Lord in the air

# THOUGHTS

# THOUGHTS

# THOUGHTS

# THOUGHTS

# THOUGHTS

# THOUGHTS

# THOUGHTS

# THOUGHTS

# THOUGHTS

# THOUGHTS

# THOUGHTS

# THOUGHTS

# Remember

whatsoever things are true,
whatsoever things are honest,
whatsoever things are just,
whatsoever things are pure,
whatsoever things are lovely,
whatsoever things are
of good report;
if there be any virtue,
and if there be any praise,
think on these things.
Philippians 4:8

You

Are

Loved

Printed in the USA
CPSIA information can be obtained
at www.ICGtesting.com
JSHW070231270624
65398JS00004B/5